Further Praise for *To Lead, Follow*

"... an aspect of leadership that every leader needs to consider."
—Sheila A. Salter, Founder & CEO, early2surg

"For those who aspire to lead others and want to take it to the next level, they need to read what Bill has written."
—Peter Jones, President, Great Lakes Forge, Inc.

"*To Lead, Follow* is an exceptional book on leadership."
—Tony Recupero, President and CEO, Recupero Consulting Group, LLC

"This is a must-read for leaders in the 21st century, especially for those who want to understand why they lead the way they lead and how they can improve their leadership abilities."
—Kirk Mansberger, CEO, Grace Bio-Labs

"Authentic and effective leadership is critically needed in this world both within and outside of organizational structures. Bill Auxier creatively tells a story that demonstrates how leadership can be modelled in all circumstances, teaching us how to be better leaders."
—Brad Slaker, Founder, DesignWise Medical Inc.
(a nonprofit corporation)

"Understanding Bill Auxier's vision of intrapersonal leadership will take a leader to greater effectiveness and success."
—George Perez, Owner, *La Jornada* Hispanic Newspaper, London, Ontario, Canada

"Taking time to reflect on the people who have influenced you, experiences you have had, and the beliefs that you hold is something that is easy NOT to do. *To Lead, Follow* demonstrates how important it is to make the time to do just that, resulting in more effective leadership."
—Sandy Henschell, Owner, Johnson Clark Printers, Inc.

"As leaders we are intently focused on the essential metrics that keep our organizations on track, particularly financial metrics. Just as important are our internal leadership metrics that keep leaders on track so we can be more effective keeping everything on track. Bill Auxier shows you how to do that."
—Aldo Ruffolo, DO, MBA, President & CEO, Lakeland Healthcare Group

"*To Lead, Follow* is a great leadership story woven throughout a son's heartwarming tribute to his father. A must-read for today's leaders who owe so much to those who shaped them."
—JOSEPH DEVIVO, PRESIDENT AND CEO, ANGIODYNAMICS

"Better leaders need to be brave enough to embrace the leadership marathon. *To Lead, Follow* will inspire you to do that."
—GEORGE TRUTZA, SERIAL ENTREPRENEUR

"Bill presents a heart-felt life story that he creatively ties into leadership development. It has helped me hone my leadership skills in a new light."
—ANDREW KOHLMANN, OWNER, IMAGE360

"Bill Auxier uniquely examines leadership; providing a fresh perspective that every business leader needs to consider."
—JIM VASKO, PRESIDENT, FOCUS MEDICAL GROUP, INC.

"A quick read on leadership that will provide long-lasting results."
—MICHAEL HLEIS, MANAGING DIRECTOR, MEDICAL & OPTICAL TECHNOLOGIES, SYDNEY, AUSTRALIA

"Reading *To Lead, Follow* and applying its concepts will create remarkable leaders and organizations."
—ERIN RECH EXEC. DIRECTOR ANALYTICS AND BUSINESS DEVELOPMENT, RIDGEVIEW MEDICAL CENTER

"*To Lead, Follow* helps leaders shore up their philosophical foundation for greater confidence and therefore greater leadership."
—WILL RUTAN, CEO, PRESIDENT, DIRECTOR, MEDERI THERAPEUTICS

"*To Lead, Follow* not only inspired me to be a more effective leader, it also inspired me to lace up and go out for a run!"
—PIERRE TWER, PRESIDENT, HEART REACH CARMEL

"Leaders who follow this advice will have greater confidence in their leadership ability and therefore be better leaders."
—JOSE R. AGUIRRECHU, RETIRED PRESIDENT, AMERICAS AT COVIDIEN

"I endorse this book as the *Best Run* lucidly narrated ... reflecting each stride eloquently ... creating a blend and balance that magnificently culminates into a leadership role at the finish line."
—RANJIT MATHEW, PRESIDENT OF MERIT GLOBAL, MUMBAI, INDIA

TO LEAD, FOLLOW

26.2 MILES TO GREATER CLARITY AND EFFECTIVENESS AS A LEADER

William R. Auxier, Ph.D.

Dynamic Leadership Academy, LLC

Copyright © 2014 by William R. Auxier, Ph.D.
All rights reserved.

www.toleadfollow.com

Printed in the United States of America
First edition, 2014

In accordance with the U.S. Copyright Act of 1976, the scanning, uploading, and electronic sharing of any part of this book without the permission of the publisher is unlawful piracy and theft of the authors' intellectual property. If you would like to use material from the book (other than for review purposes), prior written permission must be obtained by contacting the publisher at www.toleadfollow.com. Thank you for your support of author's rights.

ISBN: 978-1-5033909-7-3

Cover and Text Design by www.tothepointsolutions.com

To my dad, William L. Auxier
April 23, 1921 – May 29, 1994
Thanks, Dad!

Contents

List of Photographs	ix
Preface	xi
Introduction	1
The Starting Line	10
Mile 1	14
Mile 2	16
Mile 3	18
Mile 4	20
Mile 5	22
Mile 6	24
Mile 7	26
Mile 8	28
Mile 9	32
Mile 10	34
Mile 11	36
Mile 12	38
Mile 13	40
Mile 14	43
Mile 15	45

Mile 16	48
Mile 17	50
Mile 18	53
Mile 19	56
Mile 20	59
Mile 21	62
Mile 22	64
Mile 23	67
Mile 24	69
Mile 25	71
Mile 26	73
The Finish Line	75
The Finishing Area	78
Post-Race	80
Appendix A: Lessons Learned	85
Appendix B: My Core Values	88
Appendix C: Other Men Who Shaped My Life	90
Appendix D: A Eulogy	98
Acknowledgments	101
Reading List	103
About the Author	105

List of Photographs

Bridge Over Danube *(Jetline Action Photo)*	10
Mile 1	14
Gold Statue of Johann Strauss	16
Mile 3	18
Fountain	20
Mile 5	22
Mile 6	24
Belvedere Palace	26
Mile 8	28
Maria Theresa	34
Mile 10	36
Fountain	38
Mile 13	40
Interesting Architecture *(Jetline Action Photo)*	45
Mile 16	48
Mile 17	50
Ferris Wheel in Prater *(Jetline Action Photo)*	53
Mile 20	59
Austrian National Library	62
Parliament Building *(Jetline Action Photo)*	64
Gates of Hofburg Palace	71
Mile 26	73
Finished *(Jetline Action Photo)*	75
Finished with medal	78

Preface

The shrill ring of the telephone invaded the dark silence, penetrating my sleep. I looked at the clock. It was 2:00 a.m. I knew who was calling and why. I snatched the phone from its cradle. It was Mom. Dad's battle with heart disease was over. He had died watching the Chicago Cubs on television. It would have been better if it had been a St. Louis Cardinals game and I was there, but that was not to be.

The news was devastating. There was no way I could even consider running in the marathon I had been training for, the one that would start in only a few hours. I couldn't return to sleep. After much discussion with my wife, Elise, she encouraged me to run, reminding me that Dad would have wanted me to. So, I did.

It was Memorial Day weekend. Memorial Day had always been special in my family when I was growing up. Dad was a World War II veteran. He was also a Southern Baptist minister and a patriotic citizen. Every Memorial Day, Dad spoke at the services held in the town square of our small Southern Illinois community.

With Dad's death and the completion of my first marathon intricately entwined, Memorial Day would continue to be special.

I can't explain why, but on the tenth anniversary of his death, I felt a strong need to honor Dad by running another marathon. The obvious choice was to run the same marathon, the Bayshore Marathon in Traverse City, Michigan, which always took place on Memorial Day weekend. But I was going to be in Vienna, Austria, on business. An online search revealed that the Vienna Marathon was taking place on May 17. Why not?

The idea was hatched! I would honor Dad by running a marathon on the tenth anniversary of his passing. And not just any marathon! The Vienna Marathon would be quite the adventure in a beautiful city on another continent.

While training, I visited the Runner's World website, where I found a pace band I could print out and wear while running. The band lists what my cumulative time should be at each mile for me to monitor if I was on track to achieve my overall goal time. An idea hit me: why not break down the time line of Dad's life and substitute the target times for life events? At every mile I could reflect on a different aspect of Dad's life. It seemed like a great way to honor him.

I also decided to get a special t-shirt made that I would wear while running the marathon. I went to a local shop and purchased a plain white t-shirt. I then found an old black-and-white family photograph, one of my favorites, with Mom and Dad seated, surrounded by my brothers and sister and me when I was about eleven years old. I had what we called a flat-top haircut and I was wearing the cheapest pair of eyeglass frames available at Herrin Optical. I had the shop scan the photo and print it on the front and back of the t-shirt, with the text "Thanks Dad!" above the photograph on the front. On the back they printed "Danke Vati!" (My niece Brett had studied German in college and provided the translation.)

I was planning on running ten-minute miles. Since the race was in Europe, instead of mile markers, there would be kilometer markers; so my plan was to use the timer function on my watch and have it beep every ten minutes. At each ten-minute "break" I would focus on my surroundings and enjoy the moment and then take a photo to help me remember. For this purpose, I purchased a small fanny pack (no jokes, please) that I could fit a disposable camera in (digital cameras and smart phones with cameras were still a thing to come). My plan was to make a quick stop to snap a photograph, then I would resume running while reflecting on the aspect of Dad's life assigned to that mile. After the marathon was over, I would collect my thoughts and experiences in a journal.

Introduction

It is impossible to imagine leadership without communication. Show me a good leader and I will show you a good communicator; show me a poor leader and I will show you a poor communicator. Numerous leadership experts make a point of the importance of communication by making statements like "communication is the key to leadership" and "leadership is communication." Great leaders understand the communication process. Communication takes place on three levels: intrapersonal communication (communication with self), interpersonal communication (communication with others), and organizational communication (communication with organizations). Effective execution of all three of these levels of communication results in effective leadership.

If we accept the premise that leadership is communication, we can utilize the three levels of communication to create a leadership model consisting of three levels of leadership: **intrapersonal leadership** (the leadership of self), **interpersonal leadership** (the leadership of others), and **organizational leadership** (the leadership of an organization or organizations).

Our focus is on intrapersonal leadership—the leadership of self—which provides the foundation of which all aspects of leadership are built. A leader's ability to self-talk determines everything about him or her. Self-talk determines core values and what someone believes is right or wrong. Self-talk can enhance or diminish self-esteem. Self-talk facilitates personal growth and change. Self-talk aids in the development of alternative scenarios and outcomes through continuous learning. What you think and the words you speak are determined by the people around you and your life experiences, especially the culture in which you reside.

Intrapersonal leadership has three components: **worldview**, **continuous learning**, and **ethics**. Worldview is of particular importance to leadership because making decisions that are *not* in sync with your worldview will create inner conflict; likewise, aligning decisions with your worldview provides inner harmony. As a leader, understanding worldview will help you achieve harmony within yourself, your staff, and your organization.

Worldview's origin is a translation from the German term *Weltanschauung*. This term was used by Immanuel Kant and others as a way to denote a set of beliefs that underlie and shape all human thought and action. Wilhelm Dilthey, a nineteenth-century German philosopher, was one of the first to expound his own philosophy in terms of a worldview concept. According to Dilthey, the ultimate root of any worldview is life itself. Your worldview is yours, it may be held in common with others, but only because they are like you. Friedrich Nietzsche viewed worldview as a product of its time, place, and culture.

People aren't necessarily aware of their worldview and therefore often unaware of the origins of the philosophical foundations of their leadership styles. Studies have examined this phenomenon and determined the importance that people, life experiences, and beliefs play in the influence of leadership development. Your worldview and philosophical foundation are derived from your core values. A person's philosophical foundation for which his or her leadership is based is, therefore, a major factor of leadership effectiveness.

Worldview incorporates your assumptions—which may be true, partially true, or entirely false—to create what you believe about the world. Sometimes your beliefs are known to your conscience thought, or they might be archived in your subconscious. Sometimes you are consistent with your beliefs, at other times you are inconsistent. Regardless, these assumptions and beliefs create your perception of the world. In simple terms, your worldview is the way you address everyday issues.

Your worldview provides the philosophical foundation of your leadership ability. Every person is unique; therefore, so is your perspective of life, reality, foundation, belief system, and life experiences. Individuals may be similar, but no two are exactly alike, thus the same holds true for worldviews.

James W. Sire, author of *The Universe Next Door*, reviews the evolvement of worldview as a concept and provides the following definition:

> A worldview is a commitment, a fundamental orientation of the heart, that can be expressed as a story or in a set of presuppositions (assumptions which may be true, partially true or entirely false) which we hold (consciously or subconsciously, consistently or inconsistently) about the basic constitution of reality, and that provides the foundation on which we live and move and have our being.

In today's global society, it is inevitable that you will encounter individuals with diverse worldviews, which is why awareness of other worldviews fosters effective communication and better understanding.

Continuous learning is the connection between life experience and learning, a process identified by education scholars nearly one hundred years ago. Intrapersonal leadership and self-talk provide leaders with the opportunity to take people, experiences, and beliefs, consider what was learned, and use that information to anticipate future implications. This results in experiential learning through change and adaptation and the formation and evolution of a set of guiding principles.

Continuous learning can be broken down into a four-step process. The first step is to focus on a single event. This event can be based on a person, an experience, or a belief. The next step requires reflective thought, i.e., thinking about this event, considering it from a variety of perspectives, and writing down your observations. Next, these observations are conceptualized and analyzed into ideas and concepts. Fourth, the ideas and concepts are either totally accepted, partially accepted, or partially rejected (the same thing), or totally rejected. If an idea/concept is totally accepted, it should be embraced; likewise, if it is totally rejected, it should be abandoned. If an idea/concept is either partially accepted or partially rejected, it can be experimented with.

Experimentation means implementing the ideas/concepts, which will result in new ideas and concepts, thereby starting the process of continuous learning all over again. Continuous learning allows you to better understand your core values, your worldview, and your guiding principles and ethics. During this process, self-talk makes each step possible.

Leadership ethics refers to the principles a leader embraces to guide his or her work. The word *leadership* carries honor and prestige in our society; we assume that only ethical people are "real" leaders. Leaders adapt principles and ethics based on their respective worldview and a continuous learning process. This process does not occur in a vacuum, as ethics are a reflection of societal norms that determine moral behavior. The extent to which a leader's behavior measures up to societal standards determines how ethical he or she is.

In addition to understanding the interrelatedness of communication and leadership, effective leaders live in the present, plan for the future, and reflect on the past; the key is to balance the amount of time spent in the past, present, and future. Psychologists John Boyd and Philip Zimbardo, authors of *The Time Paradox*, provide clarity to balancing time. They break time down into five categories: 1) past-positive time perspective, 2) future time perspective, 3) present-hedonistic time perspective, 4) past-negative time perspective, and 5) present-fatalistic time perspective. Their research suggests that it is good to spend a large amount of time on past-positive thoughts and a moderately high amount of time thinking about the future and in the present-hedonistic time perspective. A minimal amount of time should be spent in past-negative and present-fatalistic thought.

I agree that a minimal amount of time should be spent dwelling on negative people and events; however, it is important to understand the lessons learned from these experiences. Dwelling on past-negative and present-fatalistic thoughts is one thing, learning from them is another. Spending too much time thinking about the past and the future prevents one from living in the present. Reflecting on the past, living in the present, and thinking about the future are essential to understanding your core values. Once again, the key is finding the proper balance.

Table 1 provides my guidelines for the amount of time effective leaders should spend in each time perspective.

Examining and reflecting on the people of influence in your life, experiences with them and others, and your personal beliefs provides understanding and clarity of core values. In turn, core values determine worldview and philosophical foundation. A good leader must first attempt to understand himself, the beginning point for all leadership efforts, and then master the skills surrounding leadership and communication with others and organizations.

Most leaders do not spend enough time thinking about the people and experiences that have influenced their lives, or why they believe what they believe. In today's need-it-now-hurry-up world, it is a challenge just to keep up, making it difficult to set aside time for reflection. While there are many activities that support reflective thought (cycling, walking, hiking, yoga, meditation, etc.), I prefer running. Peter Sagal, host of National Public Radio's *Wait, Wait … Don't Tell Me!*, wrote an article for *Runner's World* magazine titled "Voices in Your Head." In this article, Sagal, a marathon runner, talks about how runners spend a great deal of time inside their heads. He describes this as one of the best things about running, the therapeutic value of reflective thought while out for a run. I couldn't agree with him more! Practicing intrapersonal

TABLE 1

Amount of Time Leaders Should Spend in Various Time Perspectives

Time Perspective	% of Time
Past-positive time perspective	20%
Future time perspective	20%
Present-hedonistic time perspective	55%
Past-negative time perspective	> 5%
Present-fatalistic time perspective	> 5%

leadership during a run results in greater confidence and clarity, which in turn results in greater leadership effectiveness.

A marathon is 26.2 miles; running that distance requires training. Not even the most elite runners compete in a marathon without some preparation. You cannot simply wake up one morning and decide to run 26.2 miles that afternoon. Preparation is essential. Training includes running more and more miles week after week to establish a running foundation. Without that foundation, you are destined to fail.

Similarly, leadership requires a philosophical foundation, a major component of intrapersonal leadership. Some people are genetically inclined to excel at leadership, but no one wakes up one morning and decides he or she is going to be a great leader that afternoon. Like running a marathon, preparation for leadership is essential. All leaders' philosophical foundations are built upon self-talk derived from people who have influenced them, experiences they have had, and beliefs they hold—their core values. Core values provide the foundation of one's worldview—and everyone has a worldview.

When it comes to intrapersonal leadership and people who influenced me, Dad was the primary source of my core values and worldview. Dad preached in country churches around our home in Southern Illinois for as long as I can remember. He was a bi-vocational preacher, which means he did not earn enough to feed our family on his ministry alone, so he also worked for Standard Oil Company. At Standard Oil, Dad drove a truck and delivered gasoline, diesel fuel, heating oil, and other petroleum products primarily to farmers. It was tiring work.

As a Baptist preacher, Dad used a fiery rhetoric to make his point. His voice changed. He became energized. He was passionate. He delivered God's message the way he felt God wanted him to.

Dad worked hard to serve God, his family, and his employer. He put in countless hours preparing sermons, visiting the sick, and delivering fuel at any hour to help a farmer get his crops harvested in time. He did what God called him to do. It would have definitely been an easier life for Dad and our family had he not accepted God's calling to the ministry; however, ignoring God's call was not an option for him.

Dad taught me the importance of doing what is right and the importance of hard work. He taught me that you could have the most important message in the world that needed to be shared with others, but if you did not do a good job of delivering that message in front of others, the message would be lost.

My goal in this book is to share how I practice intrapersonal leadership by delving into my core values and lessons learned (inspired by my dad) so that you are inspired to examine yours. To accomplish this, I used the four-step process of continuous learning while reflecting on Dad's life as I ran the Vienna Marathon.

Remember, core values provide the philosophical foundation of your worldview, a key component of intrapersonal leadership—which guides your ability to lead.

The Starting Line

The starting line was a complicated, three-train subway ride from my hotel. I had done pretty well with public transportation in Vienna so far, but I was stressed about getting to the starting area on time. What if I got lost? What if I was late? What if, what if, what if?! All the signs were in German! I didn't know the language. I wasn't positive on which stop to get off, there were two that might work. Everything was a stress point. By the time I stepped outside of my hotel, I was anxious.

In reality, the trip to the starting line was quite simple. Once I walked down the stairs to board the subway, guess what I saw? Hundreds of other runners going to the starting line! Hundreds, maybe thousands, of people wearing running attire with Vienna Marathon race bibs pinned on the fronts of their shirts crammed and jammed themselves into the subway cars. I decided to go with the flow. Stress alleviated.

I became a follower and arrived at the starting area in no time. With my baggy running shorts, I was the obvious American. Most men wore stylish, above-the-knee spandex shorts. On top of that, most greeted new arrivals to the starting area with a one-handed salute.

Oddly, free-form urination was occurring everywhere I looked. So much for modesty! What I found more interesting than the public urination (I know, it's hard to believe there could be anything more interesting) were the people smoking. Everyone has a set of rituals they go through before a race, but I had never seen someone smoke beforehand! I about lost it when I saw one guy with his contemporary, European-style spandex shorts pulled down so he could urinate while smoking a cigarette. It was already an adventure and I hadn't even made it to the starting line yet.

Cigarettes were extinguished, pants pulled up, and a strong smell of urine wafted through the air as the throng herded toward the starting area. Runners were assigned a specific area at the starting line based on their predicted finishing time. Race bibs were color coded so people knew where to go even if they couldn't read the German signs.

It was cold and looked like it might rain. No one in the crowd spoke English. It seemed like it was taking forever until, finally, an air horn sounded, marking the start of the race. A cheer went up as everyone in my area stood with their feet planted to the street, no room to move. I started my watch when I heard the air horn, and five minutes later, after a series of shuffling and stopping, I crossed the starting line. Finally there was enough room to start an easy jog.

The United Nations building was on my right and a tall, stylish apartment building was on my left. The bridge over the Danube was just ahead, rising gradually. It was full of runners.

I decided to hop on a concrete barrier that separated the lanes of traffic on the bridge crossing the Danube to get a better view and to take my first picture. I jumped up and almost fell off. There was a large pipe running along the top of the barrier I hadn't noticed, and it made the footing a little tricky. I snapped a picture and hopped down, laughing at myself. It would be great to come all the way to Austria, to make it from my hotel to the starting line without getting lost, only to get hurt within the first mile by jumping up and immediately falling off a concrete barrier. Just like life, the beginning was exciting.

Reflection: In 1919, Lora Frances Turner (1896-1967) married George Ralph Auxier (1896-1971). A few years later, in 1921, Lora and George became parents for the first time. Dad was born in the Farmersville Store near Dahlgren, Illinois. Grandma Lora wasn't shopping, this is where they lived. Situated in the country, this general store served the area farmers.

Grandma Lora and Grandpa George lived above the store and managed it for the owner. Dad was born in a bedroom in the living quarters.

LESSONS LEARNED: Humble beginnings do not undermine success. Where you start in life does not determine where you go in life. No matter how much you prepare, there are going to be surprises. Success or failure as a leader can be determined by how you deal with surprises.

CORE VALUES: Family, love, joy, and change.

Mile 1

After nearly falling off a one-meter high concrete barrier (notice I used the metric unit of measure—very European) and running one mile (back to the American unit of measure), I crossed the Danube and passed a beautiful cathedral along the riverbank. Even though I had only run one mile, I knew I'd come a long way when I saw a traffic sign with an arrow pointing to Budapest.

Reflection: Grandma and Grandpa made ends meet by living modestly and farming in rural Southern Illinois. In 1924, Dad was three years old when his first brother, George Ralph, was born. I don't know if they still lived above the store, but if they didn't, they lived nearby as they never resided more than a few miles from the same area of Hamilton County. I think it is interesting that Uncle George, the second son, was named after Grandpa.

LESSONS LEARNED: Life is full of adventure, whether exploring new places or greeting a new life into the world. Embrace adventure, regardless of the circumstances.

CORE VALUES: Family, love, and adventure.

Mile 2

On my left was a park with a gold statue of one of Vienna's most famous residents, Johann Strauss. The statue was of Johann frozen in time playing his violin. According to my tour guide, this short, little guy was quite the ladies' man. All I could think about was the street performer who painted himself gold and posed like the statue of Johann Strauss next to St. Stephen's Cathedral for money. The ladies' man had turned into a panhandler!

Reflection: Mom was born in 1927, the third of ten children born to Georgia Ann (1901-1977) and John Randel Gholson (1895-1968). While my goal was to reflect on Dad, I couldn't ignore the fact that I wouldn't be here if it weren't for Mom too. Mom was born at home on the family farm near Broughton, Illinois. Broughton is another rural area in Hamilton County, but the other side of the county from where Dad was born.

LESSONS LEARNED: Many individuals make up a community. Your community has a strong influence on your life.

CORE VALUES: Community

Mile 3

The Ringstrasse circles around the City Centre of Vienna (also known as the Stephanplatz). St. Stephen's Cathedral (the Stephansdom) is at its center. Vienna has elegant shops; the Hofburg Palace; and many beautiful, historic buildings. As I ran by Schwartzenberg Platz I saw a cool statue of a guy on a horse. I am not sure what he had done to get a statue made in his honor, but it was impressive. There are many beautiful statues in this town.

I realized I was close to the Konzerthaus, where I attended a Mozart concert earlier in the week. At first, I resisted purchasing a ticket from the sellers who roamed the nearby streets dressed in Mozart-period costumes. I thought it looked pretty hokey, but I bought a ticket, went to the show, and thoroughly enjoyed it. What a performance—Mozart was something else. So were the Mozart chocolate, the Mozart sunglasses, and the Mozart shot glass I bought!

Reflection: Uncle Gene, Dad's third brother, was born in 1928. Dad was seven years old. Lora and George now had three boys. Knowing Dad, he was probably worried about having a new baby in the family.

One story Dad loved to tell us was about bath night. Every Saturday night, Grandma had all the boys take a bath whether they needed it or not (sorry, I couldn't resist saying it). The process was that a tub was placed on the floor by the wood-burning stove that heated the house, and then filled with water from the well that had been heated on that same stove. Each boy took a turn in the tub washing up. When Uncle Gene was around seven or eight, he was partaking in the Saturday night ritual when a family historical event took place. As he was bending over, the bare skin of his bottom made contact with the cast iron stove. As you can imagine, it was HOT! Apparently there was a raised image of a rosebud on the side of the stove where Uncle Gene's rear end made contact. From that day forward, one of Uncle Gene's best kept secrets, except among family members, was that he had a rosebud branded on his bottom.

LESSONS LEARNED: A balanced life includes making time for entertainment. Entertainment comes in many forms—from incredible musicians to old family stories.

CORE VALUES: Family and entertainment.

Mile 4

I was now west of City Centre along the Wien River. Everything looked European, like this was an area frequented by the locals and not a tourist trap. The assorted food shops were closed. It looked like a farmers market where people could purchase fresh produce and prepared food. The subway emerged from the underground along the river.

Reflection: Uncle Don, the fourth and final child of Grandma Lora and Grandpa George, was born in 1921. Dad was ten years old and in the fifth grade. He was at school when Don was born. Not long before Uncle Don was born, Dad, not realizing his mother was pregnant, told her she looked like she was getting fat. He never lived that one down. When he came home from school and learned he had a new baby brother, his main concern was how his dad was going to be able to afford another mouth to feed and another pair of shoes. Dad was a worrier.

LESSONS LEARNED: An innocent child can get away with stating an inaccurate conclusion based on observation—adults can't.

CORE VALUES: Acceptance, fairness, family, and harmony.

Mile 5

As the Wien River winds, so does the street. The river below to my left and buildings above on my right provided an endless Austrian backdrop. A stone wall separated the street and sidewalk from the river. The wall on the street side was short, the wall on the river side was a long way down. The unique architecture of the buildings, the river, the wall, the winding road—I couldn't resist. I climbed to the top of the wall, paused to soak in the scenery, took a quick photo, hopped down, and continued running.

Reflection: When Dad's younger brother George Ralph was about seven years old, he fell out of bed during the night and hit his head. Immediately after this accident, George Ralph slowly transformed into mad, animal-like behavior. Dad told me how they had to tie George to the clothesline so he could run back and forth outdoors without hurting himself or running away. How terrifying and sad it must have been for Dad and his family as they watched their son and brother's tormented life become worse and worse. Finally, in 1932, at the age of nine, George Ralph died.

It is hard to imagine what they must have felt. Dad told me how terrible this time had been and how he accompanied his mother to the funeral home to arrange for George Ralph's funeral and burial. The funeral director was showing them different caskets. Grandma Lora told him how much money she had to spend, which wasn't much, and he started directing them toward plain-looking caskets. Grandma was considering a white casket made of canvas and wood, something simple and affordable, when she pointed out a small blemish on the exterior. The funeral director boomed his reply, "Woman, what do you expect for the money you have to spend?!" When Dad told me this story, he still became angry. I was sad for him and Grandma. Now, as I remember this, my heart aches and my eyes fill with tears.

LESSONS LEARNED: There is nothing stronger than the bond and the love of family, which is always in need of nourishment. It is important to treat others with respect and dignity, regardless of socioeconomic stature.

CORE VALUES: Family, love, and dignity.

Mile 6

As I ran along the Wien River, I heard music. It sounded like a brass band. As I neared, it sounded like an Alpine genre of music that I was not usually fond of, but at that moment it sounded great. I couldn't wait to get closer to hear and see them. To prove that I run too slowly, the band had finished playing by the time I arrived. They were in uniform; so I took a photo of them anyway.

Ahead, the course took a sharp right turn at the Schloss Schönbrunn. I had the opportunity to walk the grounds of this magnificent "summer home" with over 1,400 rooms. The building's exterior was an interesting shade of yellow surrounded by incredible gardens. I stopped and took a photo of the castle. Marathon spectators, who had been taking pictures of the runners, laughed that the photo-taking had been reversed.

Reflection: Dad attended Buckingham School, a one-room building, from first through eighth grade. An open space along a country road surrounded by a few trees and bean fields is all that remains of the school today—plus the memories of those who attended. Dad was always the first student to arrive for the day. His usual routine included starting a fire in the woodburning stove that heated the large room. His reward was a hard-to-come-by candy bar from the teacher.

On one occasion, Dad accidentally caught a tree on fire. According to Dad, there was a beehive in a tree by the school, and he decided the honey and beeswax would make a tasty treat. In his attempt to smoke out the bees to harvest the sweet treat, the tree caught on fire. Fortunately, the school and students survived. I don't know how the bees, honey, or the beeswax fared.

LESSONS LEARNED: Regardless of whether a building has one room or fourteen hundred, the interactions between the people who occupy those rooms are what is important.

CORE VALUES: Community and education.

Mile 7

The course made a U-turn and we headed back toward City Centre. To my right was Auer-Welsbach Park. It looked like a nice setting for a picnic and a quiet getaway within the city. Of course, I had to admit, I thought everything looked good in Vienna today.

Reflection: The Dahlgren High School Class of 1939 included William Lawson Auxier. One of Dad's high school teachers was Mr. Foster, who I also had as an algebra teacher in high school. Mr. Foster had a unique teaching style. He could sit at his desk facing the class, and while talking, reach the chalkboard behind him and write without the slightest glance back. Dad talked about this too; so I figured Mr. Foster had honed this skill when Dad was a student.

A medal Dad kept in his desk drawer was awarded to him in high school for being an outstanding athlete. He was proud of receiving the award and playing on the high school basketball team. Dad told me how his team played in the opera house, a second-floor room above a storefront on the main street in Dahlgren. He learned to bank shots off the low ceiling to score.

Even though they had little money, Grandpa offered to pay for college if Dad wanted to attend Southern Illinois University. Dad thought it ridiculously expensive to spend $75 for one year of college tuition and room and board. He didn't want to waste the family's money.

At the age of seventeen, Dad ate roast beef for the first time. After a lifetime of pork and chicken, he said the beef melted in his mouth.

LESSONS LEARNED: Proud moments come in many shapes and sizes.

CORE VALUES: Education, recognition, pleasure, and feeling good.

Mile 8

I was close to the Wien Westbahnhof, a major Austrian railway station. The scenery had become monotonous and there had only been a few two- and three-piece bands along the way. Their music lifted my spirits. I stopped to take a picture of two guys, one playing a trombone and the other an accordion. They were having a good time.

I had always loved cobblestone streets—but not anymore! They rattled every bone and muscle in my body, from the soles of my feet to the hair on my head. I looked forward to returning to asphalt and cement streets.

Reflection: World War II had begun. Many of Dad's friends and acquaintances had either volunteered or were drafted into the military service. Dad learned that his father had been getting deferrals on Dad's behalf. After Dad found out what Grandpa George had been doing, Dad paid a visit to several members of the local draft board and asked them to disregard any deferral requests from his father. The U.S. Army drafted Dad in 1943.

Dad had never been outside of Southern Illinois. Traveling by train, he saw many states he had only read about as the train snaked its way to basic training in California.

Dad was one of many unfortunate infantrymen who trained to fight in General Patton's cavalry in the desert of North Africa but were instead shipped to the frigid Aleutian Islands in the Bering Sea off the coast of Alaska. Fully equipped in desert gear, he and his comrades were not prepared for the cold. Frostbite was a serious problem. Dad experienced it firsthand, or should I say first foot? It troubled him most of his life.

One night while on guard duty in the Aleutians, Dad saw a strange light in the sky. He promptly reported it to his superior, who blew him off. Convinced that what he had observed was important, Dad pursued officers to tell his story. He finally found a lieutenant who listened. The next day, a Japanese submarine was discovered and destroyed in a nearby bay. It was concluded that the strange light Dad saw was a search light from the submarine looking for a landing site for enemy troops and a surprise attack. Dad was promoted to sergeant.

On another occasion, Dad and his buddies were assigned a mission to invade a neighboring island. The plan of attack was kept under seal. It was expected that the U.S. Army would come under heavy resistance from an entrenched Japanese army. Instead, the Japanese had secretly departed the night before. There were a handful of casualties from nervous friendly fire. Dad later learned that the Army's top brass had expected it to be a suicide mission.

After departing the combat zone, Dad was assigned guard duty of German prisoners of war. One night, he heard a suspicious noise from behind a building and went to investigate. He found three German POWs rummaging through the garbage. One of the German soldiers spoke English well enough to communicate with Dad. Dad learned that the U.S. Army cooks, who made scrambled eggs for breakfast every day, broke all the eggs in one big batch. Rotten eggs were a common occurrence, and mixing the fresh eggs with the rotten eggs gave the entire batch of scrambled eggs a sick, rotten-egg taste. The Germans were going through the garbage because they were hungry. They were looking for food scraps to eat that weren't rotten.

As a result of this encounter, Dad was able to get the cooks to start breaking eggs three at a time into a bowl prior to adding them to the larger batch. That way, rotten eggs were eliminated from the end product. Dad was proud of this accomplishment.

LESSONS LEARNED: Some roads are better to travel down than others. You have choices, but sometimes you might find yourself headed down a path you don't want to take. As long as you have hope and faith that asphalt is out there somewhere, you can keep going. Traveling a difficult road can make you a better person.

CORE VALUES: Commitment, patriotism, duty, compassion, generosity, and honor.

Mile 9

I could tell I was almost back to the Ringstrasse because I was starting to recognize some of the statues and buildings. I found comfort in the familiarity.

Reflection: In 1946, Dad was discharged from the Army. He was twenty-five years old and, with his military experience, somewhat worldly for a country boy from Southern Illinois. He must have been lonely too, because he was looking for love.

His brother Gene helped organize youth dances in McLeansboro, the county seat. At the first opportunity, Dad went to one of the dances, proudly wearing his Army uniform. Upon entering the dance with Gene and his buddies, he met a young woman at the door, greeting all who came in. After entering, Dad quickly turned to his friends and brother to inform them that he was going to marry her. There was a slight problem though: he didn't know her name.

One of the traditions at these dances was for the young ladies to bring a treat they had made, usually a piece of pie or slice of cake, wrap it as a gift, and the young men would purchase the surprise treat, not knowing who made it. Upon making the purchase, there were two rewards: eating the treat and meeting the young lady who made it. Dad bought three different packages hoping to meet the young woman who had greeted him at the door—with no success. Being full of sweets and meeting three different young ladies, he decided the direct approach might work best. They were introduced, and a few months later, Elsie Roenia Gholson became Mrs. William L. Auxier.

Mom's dad was not excited to learn that the young man Mom had started dating was an Auxier. Apparently one of Dad's uncles had made himself known to Mom's dad in a negative way due to a relationship with alcohol. Nevertheless, Mom and Dad drove with another couple to Hernando, Mississippi, where they were married by a justice of the peace. Hernando is just across the Tennessee state line, and the closest place to Southern Illinois where getting a marriage license was a much simpler process and did not require parental signatures.

LESSONS LEARNED: Returning to a familiar place can bring comfort, even love.

CORE VALUES: Comfort, love, passion, and purpose.

Mile 10

B^{eing} back on the Ringstrasse brought familiarity and comfort. I passed the statue of Empress Maria Theresa in front of the museums across from the Hofburg Palace (where the finish line was), and the Volksgarten, then past the Parliament Building which was undergoing a face-lift. After Parliament, on the left, was City Hall, across the street, the Burgtheater. Immediately after the University of Vienna, the course turned left. The scenery was once again an architectural delight.

Reflection: George Randel Auxier was born in the summer of 1947. Mom and Dad were parents for the first time. George was named after Dad's dad, George Auxier, and Mom's dad, Randel Gholson. Dad was probably excited to start a family and at the same time concerned about their financial well-being as my parents were poor. Dad was a sharecropper and barely made ends meet. Dad was a worrier as a child and a worrier as an adult. A baby added a whole new dimension.

LESSONS LEARNED: The birth of a child brings new life to the entire family, along with responsibility.

CORE VALUES: Family, love, joy, and responsibility.

Mile 11

My watch beeped to let me know I was near Mile 11. While reflecting on Dad's life, I had been oblivious to my surroundings. I was not sure where I was. I knew the Liechtenstein Museum was somewhere nearby, and I wanted to see it. Had I already passed it? Could that be possible? Did I run right by it and not see it?

Reflection: Following the end of World War II, in the late 1940s, the Auxier family experienced a tremendous amount of change: Mom and Dad married in 1946, my brother George was born in 1947, Uncle Gene married Aunt Daphne in 1948, and Uncle Don graduated from high school in 1949.

Gene and Daphne were both from Hamilton County and the Dahlgren community. They met at a summertime community picnic. Uncle Gene, who played guitar, and a couple of his friends performed as a musical group—what I would call a "garage band," although I don't think that term had been invented yet. Another boy asked Daphne for a date during the picnic, and she agreed on one condition: he must introduce her to the guitar player in the band. Uncle Gene didn't have a chance!

Uncle Don, Dad's youngest brother, graduated from Dahlgren High School in 1949. He had already seen a lot in his life. His oldest brother was a veteran of World War II, married, and had a son. His next oldest brother died after seemingly going mad, and his other brother had just married.

LESSONS LEARNED: If you don't live in the present you miss the life that is happening around you.

CORE VALUES: Family, change, and happiness.

Mile 12

The course changed direction again and I was running alongside the Danube Canal on the City Centre side. In short order, the course had taken a bridge across the canal to the other bank, continuing in the same direction. The scenery consisted of a continuous line of old buildings, which I found pleasing to look at. I felt like I was running through a scene on an Austrian postcard. I had an inkling as to where I was.

Reflection: During the winter months of 1950, my sister, Verna Sue, was born. Mom and Dad became the proud parents of the first Auxier girl born in over eighty years. Everyone in the family was excited about a baby girl! Verna seemed too formal, so I called her Suzie; until later in life, when I called her Verna Sue. I thought Verna Sue had a nice redneck ring to it. Actually, my calling her Verna Sue was more a brother torturing his sister than anything else. If only she hadn't made me dress up in women's clothing when I was little!

A year after Verna was born, Dad's youngest brother, Uncle Don, joined the U.S. Air Force and shipped off to Korea to participate in the Korean War. Having been in the Army, Dad had a good idea of the challenges his little brother would face. I realized I didn't know anything about Uncle Don's experience in the military. All I knew was that he served his country during another turbulent time. Thankfully, Don returned home safe and sound—and Dad could stop worrying about him.

LESSONS LEARNED: Life is full of blessings and concerns; hopefully the blessings outnumber the concerns.

CORE VALUES: Family, love, and caring.

Mile 13

The course continued along the bank of the Danube Canal. When I was near the OPEC Building, I stopped to take a photograph. OPEC was a lightning rod when it came to the cost of gasoline. Crude oil prices established by the cartel wreaked havoc with everyone's budget, from Fortune 500 companies to regular people like you and me. What irony: the first time I was face-to-face with OPEC, I was using the original form of transportation instead of a gas-guzzling automobile. I noticed the 22-kilometer sign and knew I was halfway done!

Reflection: 1954—what a great year! The most significant year of my life since it is the year I was born. In May 1954, Roger Bannister was the first human to break the four-minute mile. In the days leading up to today, there was a special on television with Sir Roger Bannister, and a special ceremony in the United Kingdom acknowledging the 50th anniversary of his remarkable feat.

I was born at a small hospital in McLeansboro, Illinois, a few months after Roger Bannister made his monumental run. My parents named me William (Billy) after Dad. My middle name, Robert, was simply a name they liked; although Dad's Uncle Bob assumed my middle name came from him and he always held me in good favor.

My Great Uncle Bob married Naomi Pearce, Grandma Lora's sister. I loved his sense of humor and the interesting stories he always told. On top of that, he always made me feel special. I have no idea what his net worth was, but I thought he was the richest person I knew. Uncle Bob, also known as Bob Rawls, grew up in a one-room log cabin. Growing up poor and farming to survive, he knew what hard work was all about.

When Uncle Bob and Aunt Naomi moved to Decatur, Illinois, Uncle Bob needed a job. On his first day of job hunting, he came home with a new suit. Aunt Naomi was upset because Uncle Bob had spent nearly all of what little money they had on it. He landed a job selling furniture within the week. One of the life lessons Uncle Bob shared with me was: "If you want to be successful, you have to look successful."

Uncle Bob's hard work and desire for success paid off. He ended up owning the furniture store. One of his dress-for-success techniques was that he had two pairs of dress shoes. He would wear one pair in the morning and the second pair in the afternoon, therefore always sporting freshly polished shoes.

Uncle Bob had a plaque on a wall in his house that he loved to read to me: "Ve get too soon oldt undt too late schmart." The plaque now hangs on the wall in my office.

LESSONS LEARNED: Ve get too soon oldt undt too late schmart.

CORE VALUES: Inspiration, experience, and success.

Mile 14

Along the Danube Canal, there were more spectators near the bridges. I recognized some of them from earlier. They must have been taking advantage of the best spots to cheer on their favorite marathoner as many times as possible.

At the last intersection, a woman was loudly chanting, "Hop! Hop! Hop!" It wasn't the first time I heard this chant of encouragement and inspiration—but what the heck did it mean? These words made me think of a brown rabbit hopping around a yard, but I guessed that wasn't the intended message. My trusty book of German phrases wasn't handy; but being a bright mono-linguist, the light bulb finally went off! I had it! It didn't mean hop—it meant go. Go! Go! Go!—as in RUN!!

Reflection: The Korean War ended in July 1953. Two years later, in 1955, Uncle Don married Mary Wells, a girl from Wayne City, a small Southern Illinois town located in the next county. Don had followed in his brother's footsteps by serving in the military. Now he was following in his brother's footsteps marching down the aisle in holy matrimony.

I always liked Uncle Don. He was great working with his hands and telling stories. When I was a boy, I always marveled at all the clocks he had rebuilt and on display in his home. Each hour became a concert of bongs, dings, and cuckoos. He had a patio on the back of his house with a floor made of sandstone. I was amazed at how he had driven his pickup truck to a creek bed on a family member's farm, dug up the sandstone, put it in the back of the truck, brought it back home, and laid it down to form the floor of his patio. It seemed like he could do anything he set his mind to. On top of that, he was such a good storyteller; he could make any tale, whether it was about working on a clock or digging up sandstone, fun to listen to.

Like his older brother, Uncle Don died as the result of heart disease.

LESSONS LEARNED: Resourcefulness and creativity provide opportunity to better one's home and one's self. The ability to tell a story helps resourcefulness and creativity grow in others.

CORE VALUES: Creativity, imagination, personal development, resourcefulness, and storytelling.

Mile 15

I was beginning to see the fastest runners headed for the finish line. They were going in the opposite direction. I knew the Prater was close and I was returning to the earlier part of the course alongside the canal, except heading the other way.

Reflection: Mom and Dad's youngest child, my little brother, Anthony Wayne, was born in the summer of 1957, at Pierce Hospital in nearby Eldorado, Illinois. I vaguely remember Dad taking Verna, our brother George, and me to the hospital where we walked around the outside to see Mom through the window of her room. Mom was lying in bed holding a little bundle. I know Dad and Mom were very proud.

Tony is the name we used for my little brother. Tony was a more convenient name to sing to: "Tony boy, Tony boy, won't you be my Tony boy?" Plus Tony rhymed with bologna too, as in "Tony bolognie." We had a love-hate relationship as brothers, loving each other one minute, trying to kill each other the next.

Tony torture was a hobby that I spent a fair amount of time on. I loved trying to scare him at night. We shared a bedroom, so it was pretty easy to do with a little imagination. One time, prior to going to bed, I placed my punching bag near the side of his bed with a sheet over it. My punching bag had a floor stand with a flexible stick-like rod coming up from the stand capped with a leather inflatable punching bag. It would sway or swing back and forth from the floor. A little string attached to the rod and running to the side of my bed made it easy for me to reach down and with the flick of the wrist, a ghost could appear in the middle of the night.

Another trick that was very effective was when I took an empty metal Band-Aid box, filled it halfway with small rocks, attached a string to it, and suspended it from the bottom of Tony's bed frame. With the other end of the string by the side of my bed, a simple jerk of the string made a disturbing noise from beneath my brother's bed in the middle of the night.

The most creative scare tactic I ever used, and perhaps one of the most effective, did not involve string, just simple creativity. Right before we fell asleep, I shouted out to my little brother in an angry voice, "Tony, let go of my foot!" My little brother's shaky voice responded meekly, "I'm in my bed."

Tony is now a Baptist minister. When I have visited his church, people have always been friendly. When they find out which brother I am, they only say, "Oh, you're the one." Apparently I have provided inspiration for many of Tony's sermons. I have apologized numerous times to my brother for my transgressions and Tony has been very gracious.

LESSONS LEARNED: New life is a blessing. There is nothing like brotherly love.

CORE VALUES: Family, creativity, and forgiveness.

Mile 16

I entered the Prater, a park that consists of hundreds of acres. This land used to be the hunting grounds for Austrian royalty. Now it served the public as a huge recreation area that included an amusement park accented with a large Ferris wheel. The deep green of the trees greeted my eyes and comfy asphalt greeted my feet. At the water station, water quenched my thirst as I observed the confetti of empty water cups lying on the ground.

Reflection: When I was an infant, a viral infection nearly cost me my life. To this day, I do not know from what illness I suffered or the severity of my condition. Regardless, at this same time, my Dad's life took a pivotal turn.

Following a week-night revival church service, the Reverend Rudolph Slagg, known by most as Brother Slagg, approached Dad to speak with him privately. Brother Slagg shared a dream he had had the previous evening. In Brother Slagg's dream, Dad acknowledged and accepted God's call to preach, and once he did that, I was miraculously cured. After talking and praying with Brother Slagg, Dad accepted God's calling and became a bi-vocational Southern Baptist preacher. Immediately after announcing his intent to serve God in His ministry, I was cured. Some people questioned if this was truly an act of God or mere coincidence. For me, it didn't matter if it was a miracle or not. Dad became the man he was, sincerely serving God as best he could, and I lived to tell this story.

LESSONS LEARNED: Serving others can lead to miracles. You may wonder if they are miracles or a coincidence, that's where faith comes in.

CORE VALUES: Serving others, perceptions, and spirituality.

Mile 17

My plan to continually set my watch to beep in ten minutes seemed like a good idea, but it was one that was easier said than done. I was so deep in reflective thought I forgot to reset it the last time.

This part of the course, which I believed to be around Mile 17, was near the amusement park. The giant Ferris wheel competed with the palaces, St. Stephen's Cathedral, and the Lipizzaner horses for one's attention. There were roller coasters, games of chance, and even a Zombie ride. All of the rides were closed, probably because it was

Sunday morning or maybe because of the marathon. I had never been in such a quiet amusement park!

A street-side café was open and a few people were sitting at outside tables. A waiter wearing a white apron and holding a tray full of clear glass steins of amber beer with white frosty heads stood near the course. The beer and frothy heads sparkled through the glass. Was he offering beer to the runners? As I passed him, he looked at my shirt and yelled in English, "Thanks, Dad!"

Reflection: Some of my favorite childhood memories are of the nights spent with Dad's parents, Grandma Lora and Grandpa George. Dahlgren had a population of about 500 people, and it was a big deal when Grandma and Grandpa moved into town. Rural Southern Illinois was still behind-the-times. Moving into town brought telephone and electric service into their home—but not modern plumbing. Grandma and Grandpa had to rely on a well with a hand-pump in the kitchen, and the bathroom was an outhouse at the back edge of the property. Not too long after they moved in, Dad and others added a bathroom and indoor plumbing to the house.

It was always fun staying with Grandma and Grandpa. They had an apple tree that was great for climbing. I was treated like a king and Grandma always cooked whatever I wanted. One of my favorite foods was Grandma's fresh-cut French fries with homemade catsup. It was a sad day in 1968 when Grandma Lora died of cancer.

LESSONS LEARNED: Spending time with people older than you can be a great experience and you can learn many things.

CORE VALUES: Patience, family, and inner peace.

Mile 18

I was tired. I was still in the Prater. Everything was green and it looked the same. I had "hit the wall" a couple of miles earlier than expected. Whose idea was this anyway?

Reflection: Turning thirteen and becoming a teenager was a big deal for me, a sign of growing up. I wanted an archery set. I had shot targets on bales of hay with a friend's bow and arrows, so I knew all about their safe and proper use.

Dad decided he was going to purchase my birthday present that year, which was not the norm. When my birthday finally arrived, I couldn't wait to rip the wrapping paper off my presents. I just knew I was getting that archery set!

As I tore off the paper, I quickly realized it was a toy archery set with suction-tip arrows. Tried as I might, I couldn't mask the disappointment on my face. I quickly moved to my other present from Mom and Dad, only to find a wind-up toy.

I was disappointed, but what hurt most was the fact that Dad still saw me as a little boy. I didn't want to hurt his feelings, so I slipped away as quickly as I could and had a good cry. (I think Dad did too. My little brother ended up getting an archery set with suction-tip arrows for Christmas.)

At the same time, my older brother, George, joined the U.S. Navy. He became a Sea Bee—*a play on words,* Sea *for the letter "C" and* Bee *for the letter "B."* CB *stood for* Construction Battalion. *Sea Bees specialized in quickly building and re-building highways, bridges, runway strips, and buildings. Between 1968 and 1972, George served three tours of duty in Vietnam. As you can imagine, his deployment caused a high level of stress in our family. Prior to his third deployment to Vietnam, George was able to come home. After his seemingly short visit, when it was time to take him to the airport to say good-bye and wish him well, a married couple from the church called Dad to see if he could counsel them through some marital difficulties. Dad felt it was his duty to serve the married couple and chose to meet with them instead of going with us to the airport. I didn't learn until years later that Dad kicked himself for letting down his son and not living up to his duty as a father. Dad hoped and prayed nothing would happen to George in Vietnam. Thankfully, George was honorably discharged a few days before our sister's wedding.*

LESSONS LEARNED: Children grow up whether you want them to or not. Family comes first. Change can be difficult.

CORE VALUES: Acceptance, duty, relationships, and self-awareness.

Mile 19

A large stadium was on my left. I was only able to get a quick glance at the field. It looked like it had AstroTurf for a playing surface. I think it was a soccer stadium.

Reflection: During the summer of 1970, Dad performed his first wedding ceremony for one of his children, his only daughter. Verna married Vito Stallone on July 4 at Blooming Grove Church. Dad liked Vito, even though Vito had a Catholic upbringing and was of Sicilian descent.

Verna and Vito had met during the summer in Springfield, Illinois, where Verna had a summer job. When they met, Vito was a bank examiner for the State of Illinois. He would show up at a bank unannounced to audit their books to make sure they were in compliance with state laws. He was also a licensed pilot, so he wooed the entire family when he showed up with his airplane and offered us free rides. Vito was a handsome and hardworking man who was very nice to my sister and our family—and the free airplane rides were a definite bonus!

For her wedding, Verna and Mom worked together to cut, create, and sew her wedding dress. Even though I wasn't into clothing design, I thought it was impressive. Most of all, I will never forget how my sister fashioned her wedding veil out of a bleach bottle. This might sound a bit hokey, but I can assure you, she was beautiful! Verna and Vito's marriage was a big event for our family. On top of all that, George, who had just returned from Vietnam, walked Verna down the aisle. We all rejoiced in celebration!

The following summer, George married Glenda Davis at the First Baptist Church in McLeansboro. Glenda and George both grew up in our home town of McLeansboro, but had only gotten to know each other after George returned from his stint in the Navy. Glenda had just graduated from college and was teaching at an elementary school in St. Louis, Missouri. She was home visiting her family when she and George connected. During their dating period, Glenda had George over for dinner to meet her family. Just back from military duty, George didn't have much in the way of music albums so he asked me if he could borrow some of mine to provide contemporary music at the get-together. I gave him an assortment of albums, including **Steppenwolf Live.** *I didn't give it any thought, but George returned somewhat miffed, wanting to know why I hadn't told him about the lyrics to "The Pusher." Apparently their relationship survived the incident and Dad performed his second* *wedding ceremony for one of his children, his oldest son. Once again, our family celebrated a marriage.*

LESSONS LEARNED: Life events should be celebrated together.

CORE VALUES: Family, humor, forgiveness, resourcefulness, relationships, and joy.

Mile 20

Long, straight roads with no end in sight are not my cup of tea—but it is where I find myself at Mile 20. I thought this part of the run, through the huge park, would be a highlight. I was wrong; it was boring. While my fellow runners and I ran on one side of the road, other runners, going in the opposite direction, ran on the other side of the road. This was another turn-a-round and back segment of the course. It felt good to know I was ahead of the people running in the opposite direction; they looked pretty good, which meant I must be looking even better!

Reflection: I remember the day Mom and Dad dropped me off at my dorm at the University of Evansville, a small liberal arts college in Southern Indiana along the bank of the Ohio River. I couldn't believe I had been accepted into the School of Nursing, one of the top baccalaureate nursing programs in the country. One of the challenges I faced was the academic rigor of the program and my desire to take advantage of my newfound freedom from my parents. It was a battle of study-on versus party-on. The first couple of years, party-on won. I joined a fraternity and my social life was taken care of. Joining the fraternity certainly contributed to the party-on side of my time at the University of Evansville, but it was also a life-changing experience. The friendships made and lessons learned are still with me today. Fraternity life provided a great education. I ended up changing my major and graduated with a degree in business.

My time in college provided another type of education, an education in diversity. Growing up in rural Southern Illinois provided a homogenous environment of mostly poor, white, rednecks. At the University of Evansville, there were people from a large variety of ethnic and social-economic backgrounds, people from around the country and around the world. I also met students with different physical challenges, including blindness. Being a small school with a small campus was ideal for visually challenged students because it was easier for them to memorize the campus layout. I met students from poor families who were on need-based scholarships, and if their grades slipped, their dream of a college education would end. I met students who came from families of great wealth.

In the school of business, I met a coed from the Chicago area whose last name was the same as a major mail-order company. One day, I jokingly asked her how the catalog sales were going and she replied, "Just fine." Come to find out, she was from the family that had founded the company!

Meeting people from diverse backgrounds taught me many lessons. The education I received at the University of Evansville, both inside and outside the classroom, was priceless.

LESSONS LEARNED: Independence has a price. Education is priceless.

CORE VALUES: Independence, responsibility, challenge, adventure, discovery, diversity, education, and learning.

Mile 21

The bright note has been erased. First, the non-English speaking gentleman about my age who I was running with slowly moved ahead and pulled away from me. I could not keep up with him. The second reason is that the runners I saw a while back who were looking good and going in the opposite direction—the ones *I* thought I was ahead of—well, I was wrong. *They* were ahead of me! The people running in the opposite direction, the ones I actually was ahead of, did not look so great—they looked like I felt.

Reflection: In 1976, Dad became a grandfather for the very first time when my sister gave birth to her daughter, Brett. Mom and Dad were very proud to become grandparents. In 1979, Dad became a grandfather for the second and third time. My brother George and his wife, Glenda, provided Mom and Dad with their second granddaughter when their only child, Lori, was born. Lori's name was similar to Grandma Laura's, so it was cool having another Lori Auxier. One month later, Mom and Dad's first grandson was born when Verna and Vito's son Aaron entered this world.

Dad presided over the marriage ceremony of one of his children for the third time when my little brother, Tony, married Karen Nalley. Karen grew up in the same small town as our family, but she and Tony only came to know each other after high school. Their marriage was at Blooming Grove Church, the same church my sister was married in. I was honored to be a part of the wedding party. Tony and Karen went on to have three children: Jonathon, David, and Sarah.

LESSONS LEARNED: Embrace life's changes by being engaged with those important to you and love them openly.

CORE VALUES: Family, love, and beauty.

Mile 22

My confusion seemed to subside as we headed out of the Prater and back toward the Danube Canal. I was disappointed I did not enjoy this part of the course, and I was glad this segment was nearly over. One of my goals was to stop and enjoy the moment, to take in my surroundings at each mile. At this stage, I was having trouble doing that.

Reflection: Standard Oil made changes in its business model that would have required Dad to become a self-employed "jobber." Instead of taking on debt and financial risk, Dad retired from the company at the age of fifty-five.

Dad became a part-time pastor who did a lot of odd jobs. One of his favorite odd jobs was cutting wood. On a few occasions after working with his chain saw, Dad would notice he had a little pack pain. When he pressed his back against the corner of a door frame, the pain usually subsided. One hot summer day, after cutting wood, Dad had a more severe case of back pain and pressing against the corner of the door frame didn't alleviate it. In fact, things got worse. He finally had Mom take him to the hospital. Dad was having a heart attack!

The recurring back pain had actually been a series of mild heart attacks. Dad had blockage in three of the major vessels leading to his heart. The cardiologists referred Dad to a group of cardiovascular surgeons at Jewish Hospital in Louisville, Kentucky, who were pioneers in cardiovascular bypass surgery. Surgery was scheduled. Dad was scared and worried. We all were.

Thankfully his surgery went fine. During his recovery at the hospital, some experiences turned into family stories with staying power. Unfortunately, the pain medications Dad was receiving post-operatively were causing him to have altered perceptions of reality. For example, he thought the staples that held his incision closed were a zipper the surgeons had installed so they could "get back in" if necessary. One night, he also thought I had put a bunch of snakes in his bed. As the dosage of the medication became less and less, Dad gradually reentered the "real" world. He realized that the medications had caused him to imagine things and have bizarre thoughts. One day, he seemed depressed. When I asked him why, he explained that he had been hallucinating again. He thought he had seen Colonel Sanders from Kentucky Fried Chicken fame walking down the hall outside his room. Come to find out, Dad had, in fact, seen Colonel Sanders. He was a patient on the same floor!

LESSONS LEARNED: Listen to your body and take care of it.

CORE VALUES: Health, improvement, and self-awareness.

Mile 23

YAHOO! I have finally reached the spot where I saw the fastest runners heading back toward the finish line. Only thirty minutes to go until I reach the end! My spirits are lifted!

Reflection: Dad performed his final marriage ceremony for one of his children when Elise and I were married at the First Baptist Church of Birmingham in Birmingham, Michigan. Dad looked great in his black-tie tuxedo—but Elise took the prize for most beautiful. The pastor of the church made a few opening comments and read from Scripture, and then Dad took over. Dad's first comments acknowledged the fact that he had presided over all of his children's weddings and that ours was the last. I can't recall Dad's exact words but I know I had to choke back tears. Love filled my heart and soul.

In the two years following our wedding, Elise and I provided Mom and Dad with a granddaughter (Maren) and a grandson (Billy, the third Billy Auxier in as many generations). Maren was Mom and Dad's fourth grandchild and third granddaughter. It was no accident that Elise and I were in the Somewhere Over the Rainbow Ice Cream Parlor when Elise went into labor as we had become members of the frequent-ice-cream-eaters society during her pregnancy. After forty-eight hours of labor, Maren was finally born via an emergency C-section due to fetal distress.

The joy of becoming a parent for the first time flew out the window with my concern for Elise and Maren! It was a traumatic birthing experience, particularly for Elise, but in the end, we were the proud parents of a healthy girl. Mom and Dad drove north to Michigan after she was born and helped us with our firstborn. You could tell they were proud grandparents. When Billy was born, he had some breathing issues and was in neonatal intensive care for a few days. Fear for your child's well-being is a powerful force that supersedes all else. Fortunately, everything turned out fine.

LESSONS LEARNED: New beginnings of your own are the best.

CORE VALUES: Family, love, caring, compassion, and health.

Mile 24

The architecture indicated I was back near the Ringstrasse. I hadn't taken any pictures for a while. I was doing okay.

Reflection: In spite of not being financially affluent, Mom and Dad found a way to winter in the warmth and sunshine of Florida. Their winter home was at a campground/trailer park called Whispering Pines near Winter Haven. Our family tradition had evolved so that Thanksgiving had become an "Auxier holiday" and we all went our separate ways at Christmas time. Mom and Dad liked having their children and grandchildren gather at their home in Southern Illinois on Thanksgiving Day. Mom always cooked a feast and everyone was together, even if it was only for a few hours. After Thanksgiving Day, Mom and Dad would drive to Florida for the winter.

One year, Elise and I decided to caravan south with them to help with the long drive. As a bonus, we were going to Disney World. I drove Mom and Dad's car, with Dad riding shotgun, while Elise followed in our minivan with Mom, Maren, and Billy. We used Maren and Billy's toy walkie-talkies to communicate between vehicles. It worked on one condition, the vehicles needed to be right next to each other. We had fun making the drive and spending the night on the road.

Not far from Whispering Pines, at a toll booth, Mom and Dad's car died. We had it towed to a nearby service station, but it was going to take a day or two for the necessary repairs. We all hopped into our minivan and continued to Whispering Pines. I was glad we had driven with them.

The few days we spent with Mom and Dad at Whispering Pines was fun; more enjoyable than I had anticipated. I saw my parents in a different light with different people. Mom was learning new craft skills at the local community college and reviving her Minnie Pearl impersonation, performing at the Whispering Pines talent show and at local churches. Dad had become a serious shuffle-board player. He and Billy played for hours. Whispering Pines was full of activities that Mom and Dad enjoyed and kept them busy.

LESSONS LEARNED: Enjoy life. Identify what is important for you to enjoy life and figure out a way to make it happen. Help those you care about enjoy their lives.

CORE VALUES: Community, discovery, fun, and happiness.

Mile 25

The Waltz King was still golden, still frozen, and still playing his violin. What did women see in this guy? The spectator crowd was bigger as more and more people lined the race course. More people meant more noise, yelling, cheering, more Hop! Hop! Hop! I knew I was getting near the end. I wouldn't say I regained a spring in my step, but I did have a reenergized shuffle.

Reflection: Dad had been the pastor of Blooming Grove Church for several years, it is the church where my sister and little brother were married and where my Mom worshipped as a girl. It seemed appropriate that a ceremony honoring Dad's thirty years in the ministry was held there. Dad influenced many lives during his time in the ministry, leading congregations as a pastor, presiding over weddings and funerals, guiding people in a discovery of faith, providing comfort during difficult times, visiting the sick and elderly, and being there for others.

Even though it was a celebration in honor of Dad's service as a minister, he didn't get the day off, he was the guest preacher; which was the perfect way to celebrate. During his message, Dad acknowledged how proud he was that all of his children and grandchildren were present. In his three decades of ministry, Dad touched many lives. He was a country preacher who had not attended seminary; he was a man with a big heart and strong faith. He was a man who served God and others.

LESSONS LEARNED: Touch lives by serving.

CORE VALUES: Service, humility, and faith.

Mile 26

The streets were packed with spectators. I stopped to take a picture of the 42-kilometer marker. I was having trouble breathing—but I was almost done. I stopped again to take a quick photo of the gates of the Hofburg Palace. I could see the finish line through the gates. I was almost there. I was confused—happy—sad. Tears filled my eyes as I "ran" through the gates. It seemed like I had entered an Olympic stadium. People were everywhere. Banners! Balloons! The Hofburg! The statues! The people! The finish line! The end!

Reflection: Heart disease took its toll on Dad and depression kept a dark cloud over him during the last few years of his life. Maybe it was the medication he was on, maybe it was the toll of the disease, maybe it was age, or maybe he was simply depressed. Whatever the reason, he was not his old self the last few years he was alive. He simply didn't seem to enjoy life much. On more than one occasion, he was hospitalized with heart issues. When Elise, Maren, Billy and I moved to Northern Michigan, one of the things Dad loved to do when he visited us was to sit by himself on the beach, deep in thought, and just listen to and observe Nature. If you asked him how he was doing, his answer was usually longer and full of more information than expected. Dad's life clock was ticking, and he knew it.

LESSONS LEARNED: No matter what, there is always an end.

CORE VALUES: Acceptance, awareness, and tranquility.

The Finish Line

As I crossed the finish line, I raised my arms in triumph. Inside, I was a mess. Tears! I need air! Was I having an asthma attack? I had never had one before—Dad, it's over? It's over! Dad?

I soon realized my trouble breathing was the result of my trying to suppress a combination of hyperventilated crying and silent tears. My body and mind were exhausted. I sat down on the curb just beyond the finish line to try to sort things out. I was glad the marathon was over—but that also meant Dad's life was over. I now understood why he didn't want heroic efforts made to save his life.

Reflection: I was on a business trip when I received a call that Dad had been admitted to Welbourn Baptist Hospital in Evansville, Indiana. The situation wasn't great and Mom wanted all of us to come to Evansville. I hopped on a plane and soon my siblings and I were there. Apparently some new vascular blockage was wreaking havoc with Dad's heart. The cardiovascular physicians wanted to treat Dad with a new technique they described as a roto-rooter.

Prior to the surgery, the lead physician met with all of us one last time to review the procedure and its risks. He also wanted to let us know that Dad did not want any heroic efforts made to keep him alive if things did not go well. That got my attention like nothing before. With a smile on his face, Dad confirmed that the doctor was correct. Each of us took a turn giving Dad a hug good-bye before we left the room.

It seemed like it took forever. Finally, the same physician who held the pre-procedure family meeting came into the waiting room to tell us that all had gone well, and we could see Dad. There he was, lying on a stretcher, with multiple tubes and wires coming out from underneath the sheets. Dad was unconscious but alive, and the prognosis was good. All was well, so I bid my good-byes and headed to the airport to return home to Michigan.

The next day, a Friday, I talked with Mom on the phone. Dad was recovering in the hospital and he appreciated all of us coming to Evansville.

Saturday was the Bayshore Marathon. I had been training for months to participate in what would be my first marathon. It was going to be a day filled with big accomplishments. The marathon start time was 7:00 a.m. Mom phoned with news of Dad's death at 2:00 a.m.

LESSONS LEARNED: Giving love is the greatest gift.

CORE VALUES: Acceptance, family, faith, health, influence, love, and spirituality.

The Finishing Area

Once I realized I could breathe and wasn't dying, I got up from the curb and tried to collect myself. I slowly walked to the refreshment area. Similar to my first marathon, I had mixed feelings. I was proud of the accomplishment and reflecting on Dad's life and death had been fun, sobering, and sad.

The refreshment area was in a courtyard where a vast number of tables full of carbohydrate-rich foods, along with a variety of beverages, stood. I grabbed a bagel and cup of Gatorade and started stuffing my mouth when a woman came up to me and started speaking in German.

Using the words I had spoken most on this trip, I interrupted her, "Sprechen zie Englisch?"

She said, "Of course!" and then proceeded to tell me that she too had just finished running the marathon with a group of her friends. During the marathon, when her group came to a water station, they would all space out and go their separate ways to grab a cup of water. When finished, they always regrouped behind the guy with the "Thanks, Dad!" shirt on.

I quietly said, "Danke," as tears filled my eyes again.

As I walked away from the refreshment area, I thought about what the woman had said. Then I chuckled to myself and said, "Dad, you died ten years ago, and you're still leading others here on Earth!"

LESSONS LEARNED: A leader shapes lives, in the present and beyond.

CORE VALUES: Follow, serve, and lead.

Post-Race

I slowly started walking back to the hotel, reveling in the fact that a finisher medal hung around my neck and sober from the thoughts that had gone through my brain. I'm not sure if it was from the physical exertion of having just run 26.2 miles or the mental exertion of having just reflected on Dad's life, but I started to feel light-headed. Just then, an American symbol broke through my fogginess when I saw a pair of golden arches: McDonald's! The perfect reward!

Unfortunately, my minimal German language skill made it take longer than it should have for me to understand that the milkshake machine was out of order. A double quarter-pounder with cheese and fries along with a Coke would have to do. Running a marathon can sure help you rationalize eating junk food!

Back in the hotel, I wrote about my thoughts and experience. The next day, I flew home. A few days later, I received the photographs I had taken and went through them, journaled a bit more, and then put everything away.

I have thought about my experience often, but never talked much about it. As time passed, I felt the need to dust off my journal, the pictures, and my memories.

Reflecting on my dad's life during the Vienna Marathon provided me with the opportunity to practice intrapersonal leadership and gain clarity of my core values.

You can do the same by following these five steps:

1. Choose your method of reflection. I encourage you to run a marathon, but make sure you check with your physician first. New and veteran runners alike can find marathon-training programs at www.runnersworld.com. Other methods for reflection include cycling, walking, hiking, yoga, and meditation. Choose the one that works for you. You can also reflect on one event at a time instead of a lifetime of events.
2. Choose an event or events based on a person, experience, or belief to reflect on.
3. Reflect on that event or events from a variety of perspectives while utilizing the method of reflection selected in Step 1.
4. Identify ideas, concepts, lessons learned, core values, etc. that emerged from reflective thought.
5. Make a decision to accept the ideas and concepts that result from Step 4 or experiment with variations of these ideas and concepts starting back at Step 2, allowing them to evolve into new ideas and concepts.

As I read back through my thoughts and observations, I made a list of Lessons Learned (Appendix A) and listed the Core Values (Appendix B) in order of frequency. Looking at these lists, I heard a click in my head as a gear turned. One of my most important core values is *family*. Career and life decisions have been made based on *family*. It should come as no surprise that *family* is the most frequent core value I learned from Dad. *Family, love, acceptance, community, education, health,* and *joy* are the most frequent core values I identified in this process. I had always assumed that these values were important to me because I was such a great guy! In reality, these are core values I learned, at least in part, from Dad.

While I adopted some of the same core values Dad had, I also learned what not to do. My reflection at Mile 18 shares the story of my thirteenth birthday. Dad still saw me as a little boy while I saw myself as making the transition to adulthood. The realization that Dad and I were not on the same page was a painful experience and is painful to reflect on. I learned from this experience that children grow up whether you want them to or not and that change can be difficult. As a result, *acceptance* and *change* are core values I embrace.

Leaders must spend time in the past, present, and future, the key is finding the proper balance. Spending too much time reflecting on the past or planning the future can cause you to miss out on what is happening in the present. For example, at Mile 11, I was so deep in thought about the past that I ran right by a huge museum without even seeing it! How could I have run past a huge building without seeing it? Like I experienced at Mile 11, being too focused on the past can prevent living in and embracing the present.

Another thing I learned was the relationship between fatigue and living in the present. When fatigue was setting in, my ability to take in my surroundings and live in the present was greatly affected. At Mile 18, I realized that I "hit the wall" earlier than expected, another way of saying I was really tired. My comments are limited to five sentences with the last sentence being a negative thought that had entered my brain: *Whose idea was this anyway?* My observations at Mile 19 are limited to four sentences. Mile 21 reveals mental confusion. Fatigue hindered me from living in the present as did being totally immersed in the past.

The most significant realization I had in this process and the one thing I hope you take away from this is: your greatness as a leader depends on who you follow. The higher the quality of the leaders you choose to follow, the higher the quality of your core values and your leadership skills.

Leadership shapes lives; to lead, you must follow.

Appendix A
LESSONS LEARNED

Humble beginnings do not undermine success.

Where you start in life does not determine where you go in life.

No matter how much you prepare, there are going to be surprises. Success or failure as a leader can be determined by how you deal with surprises.

Life is full of adventure, whether exploring new places or greeting a new life into the world.

Embrace adventure regardless of the circumstances.

Many individuals make up a community. Your community has a strong influence on your life.

A balanced life includes making time for entertainment. Entertainment comes in many forms—from incredible musicians to old family stories.

An innocent child can get away with stating an inaccurate conclusion based on observation—adults can't.

There is nothing stronger than the bond and the love of family, which is always in need of nourishment.

It is important to treat others with respect and dignity, regardless of socioeconomic stature.

Regardless of whether a building has one room or fourteen hundred, the interactions between the people who occupy those rooms are what is important.

Proud moments come in many shapes and sizes.

Some roads are better to travel down than others. You have choices, but sometimes you may find yourself headed down a path you don't want to take. As long as you have hope and faith that asphalt is out there somewhere, you can keep going.

Traveling a difficult road can make you a better person.

Returning to a familiar place can bring comfort, even love.

The birth of a child brings new life to the entire family, along with responsibility.

If you don't live in the present you miss the life that is happening around you.

Life is full of blessings and concerns; hopefully the blessings outnumber the concerns.

Ve get too soon oldt undt too late schmart.

Resourcefulness and creativity provide opportunity to better one's home and one's self.

The ability to tell a story helps resourcefulness and creativity grow in others.

New life is a blessing.

There is nothing like brotherly love.

Serving others can lead to miracles. You may wonder if they are miracles or a coincidence, that's where faith comes in.

Spending time with people older than you can be a great experience, and you can learn many things.

Giving love is the greatest gift.

Children grow up whether you want them to or not.

Family comes first.

Change can be difficult.

Life events should be celebrated together.

Independence has a price.

Education is priceless.

Embrace life's changes by being engaged with those important to you and love them openly.

Listen to your body and take care of it.

New beginnings of your own are the best.

Enjoy life.

Identify what is important for you to enjoy life and figure out a way to make it happen.

Help those you care about enjoy their lives.

Leading by serving touches many lives.

No matter what, there is always an end.

A leader shapes lives, in the present and beyond.

Appendix B
MY CORE VALUES

To get an understanding of what my core values are, I reviewed my notes from the marathon journal. The results are:

Core Value	Frequency
Family	14
Love	9
Acceptance	4
Community	3
Education	3
Health	3
Joy	3
Adventure	2
Caring	2
Change	2
Compassion	2
Creativity	2
Discovery	2
Duty	2
Faith	2
Forgiveness	2

Core Value	Frequency
Happiness	2
Honor	2
Relationships	2
Resourcefulness	2
Responsibility	2
Self-Awareness	2
Serving Others	2
Spirituality	2
Awareness	1
Beauty	1
Challenge	1
Comfort	1
Commitment	1
Dignity	1
Diversity	1
Discovery	1
Entertainment	1
Experience	1
Fairness	1
Feeling Good	1
Follow	1
Fun	1
Generosity	1

Core Value	Frequency
Harmony	1
Humility	1
Humor	1
Imagination	1
Improvement	1
Independence	1
Influence	1
Inner Peace	1
Inspiration	1
Leading	1
Learning	1
Passion	1
Patience	1
Patriotism	1
Perceptions	1
Personal Development	1
Pleasure	1
Purpose	1
Recognition	1
Service	1
Storytelling	1
Success	1
Tranquility	1

Appendix C
OTHER MEN WHO SHAPED MY LIFE

Many people have influenced me; some I knew and others I did not. They include: Mrs. Elliott, my eighth-grade English teacher; Miss Schwarm, my twelfth-grade English teacher; several college professors; my mother; my wife; my children; other relatives; Mother Teresa; Abraham Lincoln; John F. Kennedy; Martin Luther King, Jr.; Ronald Reagan; and Willie Mays.

ABRAHAM LINCOLN

Abraham Lincoln was a great man who did great things. His words speak to me. His first political speech occurred in Pappsville, Illinois, in 1832. Following a long dissertation by his opponent, Lincoln's speech contained seven sentences, the first two being "Fellow citizens, I presume you all know who I am. I am humble Abraham Lincoln."

From all accounts, Abe Lincoln was a humble man, reinforced by his words, "My early life is characterized in a single line of Gray's *Elegy*: "The short and simple annals of the poor."

These quotes from Abraham Lincoln also inspire me:

All that I am or hope to be, I owe to my angel mother.

Truth is the best vindication against slander.

Writing, the art of communicating thoughts to the mind through the eye, is the greatest invention of the world.

As I would not be a slave, so I would not be a master. This expresses my idea of democracy.

I never encourage deceit; and falsehood, especially if you have got a bad memory, is the worst enemy a fellow can have …

I can make a brigadier-general in five minutes, but it is not easy to replace a hundred and ten horses.

My father taught me to work, but not to love it. I never did like to work, and I don't deny it. I'd rather read, tell stories, crack jokes, talk, laugh—anything but work.

Lincoln could compress the most words into the smallest space to clearly explain an idea. He could say more in fewer words in an elegant pattern of carefully chosen words. A perfect example is the Gettysburg Address.

In November of 1863, President Lincoln was invited to make a few remarks at the dedication of the cemetery at Gettysburg. Thousands of men had been killed in battle at this site, and their bodies had been hastily buried with little time spent identifying them. Their bodies were being re-interred. The speaker for this occasion was Edward Everett, former president of Harvard College, former U.S. Senator, and former Secretary of State. It was expected that Mr. Everett's speech would be quite lengthy, which it was.

According to myth, President Lincoln wrote his speech on the train to Gettysburg on the back of an envelope. In fact, he worked on the speech for weeks. He was having trouble with the ending, and shortly before he left for Gettysburg, he told a colleague that he was about half done with his address. He must have had the rest in his mind as it only took a few quiet minutes to write it all out.

Everett's speech lasted two hours. Lincoln's speech contained 272 words, and was over before a photographer could set up his camera and take a photograph. Immediately following Lincoln's address, some considered it a failure. As his words hit the newspapers and reached the general public, the Gettysburg Address made a deep impact. As reported in the *Chicago Tribune*, "The dedication remarks by President Lincoln will live among the annals of man."

THE GETTYSBURG ADDRESS
Fourscore and seven years ago our fathers brought forth upon this continent a new nation, conceived in liberty, and dedicated to the proposition that all men are created equal. Now we are engaged in a great civil war, testing whether that nation, or any nation so conceived and so dedicated, can

long endure. We are met on a great battlefield of that war. We have come to dedicate a portion of that field as a final resting-place for those who here gave their lives that that nation might live. It is altogether fitting and proper that we should do this. But in a larger sense we cannot dedicate, we cannot consecrate, we cannot hallow this ground. The brave men, living and dead, who struggled here, have consecrated it far above our poor power to add or detract. The world will little note, nor long remember, what we say here; but it can never forget what they did here. It is for us the living, rather to be dedicated here to the unfinished work which they who fought here have thus far so nobly advanced. It is rather for us to be here dedicated to the great task remaining before us, that from these honored dead we take increased devotion to that cause for which they gave the last full measure of devotion; that we here highly resolve that these dead shall not have died in vain; that this nation, under God, shall have a new birth of freedom, and that government of the people, by the people, and for the people, shall not perish from the earth.

Abraham Lincoln taught me honesty, humor, to never give up, to do what is right, the importance of family, and to look to God for guidance.

JOHN F. KENNEDY

In November 1960, I turned six years old and John F. Kennedy was elected President of the United States. I remember watching President Kennedy's inaugural address on a small black-and-white television with my parents and brothers and sister. Even the grainy images being transmitted into our living room could not hide the pomp and circumstance of the event. It was very exciting.

When JFK said, "And so, my fellow Americans, ask not what your country can do for you—ask what you can do for your country," he struck a chord with me. His words penetrated my soul.

What a compelling question and frankly, what a challenge. What can one person do? The answer I came up with is to take advantage of the opportunity! An infinite number of possibilities exists: work, play, worship, helping others, serving others, teach, marry, raise your children, feed the poor, build an empire, dig a ditch, become a millionaire, get elected, lead, farm, serve God, volunteer ... anything and everything you do can help or hurt your country.

President Kennedy reinforced the importance of public speaking and self-reliance to me.

WILLIE MAYS

In 1954, two major events occurred: I was born and Willie Mays made his famous over-the-shoulder catch in the World Series when the New York Giants beat the Cleveland Indians in four straight games. Willie Mays grew up in Alabama, where his father worked in a steel mill. His father played semi-professional baseball on a team the mill sponsored. Willie's high school did not have a baseball team, so he played other sports. At the age of sixteen, Willie began his professional baseball career, playing for the Birmingham Black Barons in the segregated Negro Southern League. While his parents supported his baseball dreams, they insisted he graduate from high school. Willie only played in the home games so he would not miss class. The day he graduated high school, he was signed by the New York Giants.

Mays got off to a rocky start in the majors, going hitless his first twelve times at bat. Unlike other major league managers, who might have benched the rookie or sent him back to the minor league, the Giants' Leo Durocher had faith in his young center fielder. That faith paid off when Mays broke his hitless streak by blasting a home run over the left-field roof. After another hitless thirteen at bats, Mays got his second major-league hit. Before the season was over, he had nineteen home runs. His spectacular fielding was making headlines, especially a catch he made that season against the Pittsburgh Pirates. A long fly ball was hit into the outfield. Mays raced across the outfield and caught a 475-foot drive with his bare hands! His performance paced the team for the rest of the season, resulting in the Giants winning the National League pennant that year.

Willie Mays had 7,095 putouts as an outfielder—an all-time record. His career batting average was .302. He drove in more than one hundred runs a year in eight different years. His 660 home runs placed him in the top ten for all-time home runs, even to this day. He won the Gold Glove award twelve times. He was voted Most Valuable Player in the National League in both 1954 and 1965. And, in 1979, he was inducted into the Baseball Hall of Fame.

As a centerfielder in little league baseball, I wanted to be just like Willie Mays; after all, we not only played the same position, our first names were similar. People laughed when I said I wanted to be just like him. What I did not realize at the time was that many people laughed because they thought it was funny I wanted to be like a black man.

Willie Mays taught me two things: do what you love and color blindness.

Ronald Reagan

In the summer of 1987, Ronald Reagan spoke to the people of West Berlin, Germany. While he was talking, the people of East Berlin, separated by the Berlin Wall, could also hear President Reagan's words. Reagan spoke of freedom, and how a wall encircled the free sectors of a city. He directed many of his comments to General Secretary Gorbachev, head of the Soviet Union. About midway through his speech, President Reagan uttered these now famous words:

> General Secretary Gorbachev, if you seek peace, if you seek prosperity for the Soviet Union and Eastern Europe, if you seek liberalization: Come here to this gate! Mr. Gorbachev, open this gate! Mr. Gorbachev, tear down this wall!

It was a bold move for President Reagan to speak those words. Less than a year later, the Berlin Wall was demolished.

President Reagan taught me the importance of doing

what is right even when it falls in the face of not being politically correct. He also taught me that a public speaker who chooses his words properly and delivers those words in a compelling and persuasive fashion can change the world.

Martin Luther King, Jr.

Martin Luther King, Jr., taught me the importance of being an effective communicator. He could make words sing! He too stood up for what he thought was right in the face of great uncertainty and peril. I will always remember the words he spoke the night before the world was robbed of him:

> Like anybody, I would like to live a long life. Longevity has its place. But I'm not concerned about that now. I just want to do God's will. And He's allowed me to go up to the mountain. And I've looked over. And I've seen the Promised Land! I may not get there with you. But I want you to know tonight, that we, as a people, will get to the Promised Land! And so I'm happy tonight. I'm not worried about anything. I'm not fearing any man! Mine eyes have seen the glory of the coming of the Lord!

Appendix D
A EULOGY

I wrote this eulogy and read it at Dad's funeral service:

In Memory of William L. "Bill" Auxier

Bill is the greatest name there is.

As a boy, one of my favorite stories was *Three Billy Goats Gruff*.

As a boy, I was always trying to talk Mom and Dad into letting me have a billy goat, and could not understand why they laughed when I tried to persuade them with the argument that I could sell the billy goat's milk.

As a boy, I loved to pretend I was a cowboy along with my heroes Billy the Kid, Buffalo Bill, and Wild Bill Hickok.

As a boy, I loved to play baseball like my hero Willie Mays.

As a boy, I wanted to grow up to be a Standard Oil man, a preacher, a comedian (especially one like Red Skelton), and a professional baseball player (but only a St. Louis Cardinal), and I shared these dreams with my dad, Bill.

As a man, I loved it when I was no longer Billy and became Bill.

I love my mom, Elsie, who fell in love and married a country boy from Dahlgren named Bill.

I love my brothers, my sister, my sisters-in-law, and brother-in-law; their children, my nieces and nephews, and their dad, their father-in-law, their Grandpa Bill.

I love my wife, Elise, who fell in love and married a small town boy from McLeansboro named Bill.

I love my children, my daughter, Maren, and my son, Billy.

As a boy and as a man, I love the name Bill, and I love my dad.

There is no greater honor than to share the name, be it a first name or last, with someone you love.

Acknowledgments

I am grateful to many people who made this book possible.

My mother and my dad's brothers, Uncle Gene and Uncle Don, have all passed since I ran the Vienna Marathon and prior to me writing *To Lead, Follow*. They provided historical details I used for my reflective thinking during the marathon, and they supplied their stories with great love and joy. I am grateful to them for many things, in addition to their stories.

Elise, my wife, and our children, Maren and Billy, endured my training and planning to run the Vienna Marathon, in addition to my painful creative writing process.

Most of all, I acknowledge the inspiration and talent of Mary Jo Zazueta, whose guidance made this possible. It all started when I attended her free seminar at the University Center on how to publish a book. I didn't know it at the time, but attending that seminar helped make one of my dreams come true. Thank you, Mary Jo!

Reading List

Bingham, J. (2002). *No Need For Speed: A Beginner's Guide to the Joy of Running*. Emmaus, PA: Rodale.

Bingham, J. and Hadfield, J. (2003). *Marathoning for Mortals: A Regular Person's Guide to the Joy of Running or Walking a Half-Marathon or Marathon*. Emmaus, PA: Rodale.

Hamilton, F. and Bean, C. (2005). "The importance of context, beliefs and values in leadership development." *Business Ethics: A European Review* 14(4), 336-347.

Heslam, P. (1998). *Creating a Christian Worldview: Abraham Kuyper's Lectures on Calvinism*. Grand Rapids, MI: Eerdmans Publishing Company.

Hollander, E. and Julian, J. (1969). "Contemporary trends in the analysis of leadership processes." *Psychological Bulletin*, 71(5), 387-397.

House, R. (2004). Illustrative examples of GLOBE findings. In House, R., Hanges, P., Javidan, M., Dorfman, P., and Gupta, V. (Eds). *Culture, Leadership, and Organizations*. Thousand Oaks, CA: Sage.

Kluback, W. & Weinbaum, M. (1957). *Dilthey's Philosophy of Existence: Introduction to Weltanschauungslehere*. New York: Bookman Associates.

Naugle, D. (2002). *Worldview: The History of a Concept*. Grand Rapids, MI: Eerdmans Publishing Company.

Sire, J.W. (2004). *The Universe Next Door: A Basic Worldview Catalog (4th ed)*. Downers Grove, IL: InterVarsity Press.

Smircich, L. and Morgan, G. (1982). "Leadership: The management of meaning." *Journal of Applied Behavioral Science*, 18(3), 257-274.

About the Author

Bill Auxier is a contributing author to the *Wall Street Journal* bestseller *Masters of Success: Proven Techniques for Achieving Success in Business and Life*, and founder of the Dynamic Leadership Academy. He helps leaders develop and understand their personal definition of leadership for greater personal and organizational success by utilizing what he has learned in the real world, combined with what he has learned in the academic world.

In the real world, Bill worked his way up from the bottom to become CEO of a global medical device manufacturer; in the academic world, he earned his doctorate in leadership.

After raising their family in Traverse City, Michigan, Bill and his wife, Elise, are empty-nesters enjoying the sunshine and warmth of Tampa, Florida.

To access free content Bill has developed on leadership, please visit his website:

www.billauxier.com

www.ingramcontent.com/pod-product-compliance
Lightning Source LLC
Chambersburg PA
CBHW051723170526
45167CB00002B/773